Illegitimacy:
The Battle Over
Your Identity

ENDORSEMENTS

Illegitimacy performs DNA repair on the Kingdom! Ryan Johnson has unveiled the KEY to advancing sonship! By exposing the spirit of illegitimacy, this book will empower sons and daughters to throw off the cloak of false identity and take their place in the Kingdom of God.
– **Apostle Sherri Ezzell**, Founder of GroundBreakers Regional Prayer and Revival Hub, Tribe Network Senior Leader

Ryan Johnson shares the heart of God in this life-changing book. Nugget after nugget of wisdom sounding the alarm on identity issues, while releasing insight to the illegitimate, leaving millennials and people of all ages that have questions on sonship receiving not only their answers but deliverance and healing at the same time! This a must read!
– **Apostle Theresa R. Hawkins**, iHUB-York, PA

From the moment Prophet Ryan Johnson sensed the prophetic call on his life, he has pursued God with everything in him. He is God's man, my close friend, and a rising voice to this generation. This book will challenge you to embrace your God-given identity, and you will have a better understanding of how God operates after reading it.
– **Dr. Ronnie Phillips, Jr.**, Lead Pastor of Abba's House, Chattanooga, TN

One of the greatest tactics of the enemy is to either steal or confuse the identity and legitimacy of an individual. As long as the enemy can keep you questioning who you are, you will never walk in the authority of an heir. Ryan Johnson masterfully communicates the blessing of sonship. *Illegitimacy: The Battle Over Your Identity* gives prophetic insight into the battle over our identity. It peels back the veil of deception and exposes the spirit of

Illegitimacy. You will learn from this book that your identity is not what life has dictated to you or what society has told you. You will gain life-changing insight into the truth that you are who God says that you are!
– **Andrew Towe**, Lead Pastor of Ramp Church Chattanooga

Jesus came to give us a new identity – a new life. The enemy wants to blind us from who we are in Christ, so he can make our life a hell on earth and steal our eternal rewards. You have authority. You have power. You have influence. But if you don't understand who you really are, you will never walk in the anointing He's given you to impact the world around you. In *Illegitimacy*, Ryan Johnson shines light on the subtle deceptions the enemy uses to keep you in the dark about your value, worth – and identity – in Christ. This book will empower you to step into the fullness of what God has called you to be and do for His glory. Get ready for a revolutionary encounter as you read the pages of this manuscript.
– **Apostle Jennifer LeClaire**, Ignite Network, Awakening Blaze Prayer Movement

I could not think of a better person to steward this revelation than Ryan Johnson. Get ready for your heart to be challenged as Ryan gives explanation to social and theological thought process that proves our need to know God as father. Ryan does an excellent job at walking the reader through their identity as sons and daughters of God and avoiding the pitfalls of the devil. This book is a timely word from God that will truly bless the body of Christ. – **Apostle Johnathan Stidham**, Ignite Church Nicholasville

This book is a must-read! Ryan reveals the strategy of the enemy to pervert and steal the identity that God wants to release within sons and daughters. Furthermore, Ryan eloquently details the revelation of who we are called to be as sons and joint-heirs with Christ. As you read this, any hold that illegitimacy has had on you will be broken. Ryan releases the reader to run in their God given identity. You will find freedom and purpose as you read this powerful book! – **Pastor Joshua Gay,** High Praise Orlando

Illegitimacy:
The Battle Over
Your Identity

RYAN B. JOHNSON

DEDICATION

I would like to dedicate this book to my beautiful wife, Kristi, for her constant support and encouragement to the fulfillment of my dreams. Kristi, you are truly my best friend in this world, and I am grateful for the life that we have together. We have grown up together, and we shall see the best years of our lives because we do so together!

I also dedicate this book to my four children as a reminder to dream big and wild. Never limit yourself within the world you live in, rather let the world around you experience the dreams that are within you.

Finally, I want to tell my parents how much I love and appreciate the support that they have shown me, my family, and my siblings. There has never been one day that has gone by that I did not understand how much you cared, loved, and supported us in our adventures throughout life. Your life has been an inspiration and constant reminder to never quit!

CONTENTS

Preface   xi

Chapter 1: The Vision   1

Chapter 2: Anointing of a Son   11

Chapter 3: A Son's True Identity   21

Chapter 4: Are You the Son?   31

Chapter 5: The Cross of Identity   39

Chapter 6: Identity Battles and Struggles   49

Chapter 7: More than a Christian   57

Chapter 8: Keys to the Kingdom   63

Chapter 9: Embracing the Father's Identity   71

Chapter 10: Your Destiny Awaits   79

About the Author   87

References   89

PREFACE

During the presidential campaigns for the election of our 45th president, I found myself grieving over what I was witnessing through leaders. Not political leaders, but rather many different Church leaders. From pastors, teachers, prophets, apostles, evangelists, deacons, and directors, you name the leader, I was witnessing something that was absolutely ripping my heart out for a generation. As the elections drew to a close and then into the following weeks after the election, I read post after post after post where leaders used social media as a platform to rip into those they disagreed with. I read status updates of Church leaders who called millennials such names as "snowflakes," "whiners," "spoiled brats," "garbage," "lazy," "tantrum throwers," and the list could go on. These leaders declared statements such as, "These good-for-nothing, lazy, whining crybabies need to quit protesting and go get a job." Even quotes like, "They're still crying, pouting whiners. Suck it up, Buttercup! We didn't soil our pants and suck our thumbs when BHO [Barrack Hussein Obama] was elected!" "Whiners, crybabies, and deadbeats will have to get real jobs or live with mommy. Your free ride is over!"

I found myself hurting for a generation of young people that I had never met. But the grieving did not just stop with them as I soon discovered that it was bigger than a younger generation. This was a problem across all generations. Age had nothing to do with it; it had everything to do with our identity as a son. I wanted answers as to why I was witnessing what so many leaders were doing to individuals. Although I did not agree with what many people were doing with their protest of the elections or political candidates, I just couldn't bring myself to belittle those people in ways that other Church leaders were easily doing.

Throughout the beginning of time, generations have always found fault with other generations. This isn't anything necessarily new. As time goes on, we will have problems with the ideas or actions of those before and those behind us. It is the nature of our flesh to want to have personal issues in those we disagree with. We must learn to grow in open conversation and have a sincere desire to personally allow ourselves to be challenged with truth. No generation is the perfect generation. Therefore, no generation has all the answers. The best that can come out of it all is when we learn that we are ONE generation through Jesus.

Though grieved, I began to take this to the Lord more in prayer as I sought the answer to what was happening. *God, why are so many in the Church being so vicious in their rants towards those who disagree with them?*

I could envision them crushing individuals on social media, and then seeing those same people in public with an invitation to their church services – criticizing them on social media platforms, but describing to those individuals about how much they loved them and wanted them to attend their services where the love of God was tangible. How easy it is to belittle others through a media platform and offer a cheap invitation during the week! But as I can easily see that, I can also see those individuals not buying into those cheap offers. Millennials and other generations are no longer buying the cheap talk of "Jesus loves you, and we love you," when they can see how you really feel about them. Though this is the case, it is scary to realize that many of these leaders just don't see what they are doing.

"You forfeit God's love as soon as you get fascinated with the world (1 John 2:15). God wants you to move into fullness. He wants to move you into the place where you're steadfast

and unmovable and always abounding in the love of God. Only a risen, exalted Christ can make that possible. He's got to have pre-eminence in my living... in my thinking... in my time... in my language... in all things, not some things. Every day (every second) should be holy for a man who has the Holy Ghost."
– Leonard Ravenhill

"Darkness cannot drive out darkness; only light can do that. Hate cannot drive out hate; only love can do that."
– Martin Luther King, Jr.

Chapter 1
THE VISION

"What you focus on – the kingdom you're aware of – is what you release into the atmosphere around you. You're actually influencing your surroundings by what's going on inside. The world is filled with unbelief and sin and so many horrible things. The kingdom of God is filled with perfect trust and peace. You will always reflect the nature of the world you're most aware of."
– Bill Johnson, Bethel Church

It is my sincere desire to see the Church (Ekklesia – legislative governing body) become the best that we can possibly be. I realize that it is also the desire of so many, and yet we often find ourselves walking in division more than unity. There is a real enemy out there that is not flesh and blood. For us to act like there isn't a spiritual warfare from the enemy's (Satan's) camp is to keep denying rather than advancing beyond our constant issues, problems, and strongholds. The goal is to become better than yesterday in our personal walk with the Lord – to increase in wisdom, knowledge, and understanding. We want to be encouragers of one another, regardless of generation, skin color, male, or female.

While in my time of prayer, I began to become focused on what was the root to this division that was so evident in the Body. That is when the Lord shared a vision with me. In this vision, the Lord reminded me of a specific time where I was a little boy with my dad, as he was taking the time to talk to me. In the vision, my dad was doing what he had always done. Before I can share this part of the vision, I need you to understand that my dad is a Disabled American Veteran (United States Air Force). Because my dad is a 100% DAV, he has had limits placed on his physical ability to do certain things. It was because of these limitations that he raised my siblings and me in a different manner than most. I was raised with a dad who was more of a John Wooden type figure in my life. He physically couldn't get out and do all the sports that a lot of dads could do with their children. Yet, with my dad, it was a constant pep talk.

In this vision I was seeing and hearing everything that I had heard while growing up. I saw my dad talking to me when I was about 8-10 years old. He was saying, "You can do this. You will win, because my son is a winner. You won't quit, because my son is not a quitter; he is a winner. No matter what you do, you will be successful, because you are my son." Those are the type of things that I heard my dad speak into me while growing up. I knew no different.

As the vision forwarded, I soon saw another father with a son, both of whom I had never seen before, who were now in a conversation, but it would not be like the one with my dad and me. I could immediately tell that the dad was speaking pretty hard to this little boy, and it wasn't words of encouragement. That's when the vision brought me closer to them and I heard the dad say, "You are such a huge disappointment to me. Can't you do anything right? Why do you have to keep messing up everything that you do? I don't want anything to do with you. You are an embarrassment to me." Then the vision was over.

Immediately I went back into prayer asking God what I had just seen and why. The Lord spoke to me that what I had seen was a glimpse of how the Church has been speaking into others for some time now. The father who was treating his son with anger, frustration, bitterness, hatred, etc., was a type and shadow of how many in the

Church have been speaking into those whom we should be raising and equipping. Sadly, we have developed leaders in the Church today who focus more on the wrong things rather than raising up sons. We have leaders who are determined to keep others in a place that they need them to be, rather than for them to step into the destiny of their purpose. When the Lord gave me this vision, my next question was simple: "What is happening, and why has this become the case?"

The Lord then said something that forever changed me. He said, "There is a spirit of illegitimacy that has been active for some time now, but has greatly increased over time."

ILLEGITIMACY! What? I have never heard of the terminology about a spirit of illegitimacy. The second that I speak about this kind of spirit, it will immediately open the door to every critic out there. After all, it's not like I can direct you to the exact book, chapter, and verse where Jesus spoke about the spirit of illegitimacy. And, let's face it, most of us will immediately think of the understanding of illegitimacy with being a bastard child. How in the world could God be saying something about a spirit that has created a lot of the problems that we have with others?

The Lord then began to reveal to me how the spirit of illegitimacy has been effective for so long and what illegitimacy does to others.

Therefore, I want to encourage you, that as you read this book, to take in what the Lord is revealing to you personally. Don't read this book as if it were the latest book on the market and it's just another good read. Take the time to invest in what God is showing you individually. As you read, I believe that when you complete this book, you will position yourself to receive your *purpose* as a *son* and not as an illegitimate child.

> So, you have not received a spirit that makes you fearful slaves. Instead, you received God's Spirit when He adopted you as His own children. Now we call Him, "Abba, Father."
>
> – Romans 8:15 (NLT)

One of the earliest things that we all learn about the enemy (Satan), is that he is incapable of creating anything. Satan does not create, he can only manipulate or pervert what is already in the natural or supernatural. In the late nineties, a company (BASF) used a campaign for their commercials with the declaration, "We don't make the things you buy, we make the things you buy better." With that in mind, let us think of Satan as having that mentality of a catch phrase,

"Satan doesn't make things, he takes the things that God created, and makes them to appear to be worse."

You must never lose sight that Satan cannot create anything out of nothing. There has to be some kind of substance that is already established in order for him to manipulate or pervert that reality into his weapon. God created angels and spoke light into existence, and yet, Satan has appeared as an angel of light (2 Corinthians 11:14). God is defined as a roaring lion, and yet Satan is described *as* a roaring lion (1 Peter 5:8). There are plenty of examples that I could use, but I hope that you understand what I am stating without going into great detail.

With the understanding that Satan can only manipulate and pervert, we then have to accept that within the structure of a spirit realm. For example, we know that joy is from the Lord, and to counteract that the enemy comes with a spirit of depression. We know that peace is from the Lord, while the enemy comes at you with a spirit of contention or strife. We know that Jesus is the Christ, the Anointed One. And, we also know that Satan has active on the earth an antichrist spirit. For everything that God has for you, the enemy has his perversion in order to break you down.

With all of that said, I do want to stretch your thinking a little bit here. When we see someone who has a drinking problem, or a drug problem, or a pornography problem…we quickly say that they have a spirit of addiction. We all agree that this is obviously taking place, but have we thought about how and why addiction is the work of the enemy? Remember, he cannot create, only manipulate or pervert what is already established from God. What if you realized that addiction was never meant for what the enemy uses it for, but in reality, God wanted you to be addicted? You see, God wants you addicted to His presence, His glory, His grace, His love, etc. Addiction is there for you to become so addicted to God that you cannot live without Him. You don't want anything but Him. The enemy has taken this and manipulated it in a way that instead of our addiction to the Father, he replaced that with drugs, alcohol, pornography, and so forth. The enemy has used crystal meth (other drugs as well) and made it a god for people. Once they tasted the drugs, they were hooked. At this point, the enemy knew that they would do anything they could to be back in the presence of their god (meth). Nothing else mattered but getting back to that certain god (drug, alcohol, sex, etc.). Though the enemy can pervert or manipulate that, God established the reality of addiction.

O taste and see that the Lord is good;
How blessed is the man who takes refuge in Him!

– Psalm 34:8

Blessed are those who hunger and thirst for righteousness, for they shall be satisfied.

– Matthew 5:6

Granted, I do acknowledge that we have the tendency to give too much credit to the enemy and not enough to the Father. At no point in this do I want to come across with the idea that the enemy is greater than the Lord. The enemy is a defeated foe, but a foe who does attempt to overthrow the identity of those in relationship with the Father through the Son, Jesus Christ. We cannot simply act like the enemy doesn't attempt to come after those who are in Christ. God is always greater than anything that the enemy can throw in our faces. And yet, there is a daily reminder that many who profess to have a relationship with the Father can become victims to the deception and manipulation of the enemy. It is easy to allow the tricks of the enemy to overcome us in such a way that we fail to remember and respond from the place of victory. Then there come the times that we blame God for what isn't happening without the understanding as to how the enemy works.

"The enemy doesn't care how many days you live as long as you don't live in the days you have."
– T.D. Jakes

In those times of walking in our lack of understanding, we easily believe that we will never accomplish certain things, or that our dreams will never become our reality. We are too quick to think that God made a mistake at the very moment when He made us, that He didn't give us the ability to fulfill the desires of our hearts. It really is amazing how we can come up with more excuses to why it's not happening and why it will never happen for us. We act like God only created a select few individuals for His greatness, and we can reason why He only created us to be minions on this earth – only taking up space with no real goal in our lives. Sadly, we have the tendency to believe and often convince ourselves that God has made a huge mistake. We have this unique ability to come up with a thousand different reasons to why we cannot fulfill the destiny of our lives. Regardless of the color of skin, social status, physical location, or nationality, I have yet to meet anyone that wasn't created with a divine purpose for the Glory of God.

For we are His workmanship, created in Christ Jesus for good works, which God prepared beforehand so that we would walk in them.
– Ephesians 2:10

Oh yes, You shaped me first inside, then out; You formed me in my mother's womb. I thank You, High God – You're breathtaking! Body and soul, I am marvelously made! I worship in adoration – what a creation! You know me inside and out, You know every bone in my body; You know exactly how I was made, bit by bit, how I was sculpted from nothing into something. Like an open book, You watched me grow from conception to birth; all the stages of my life were spread out before You, the days of my life all prepared before I'd even lived one day.

– Psalm 139:15-16 (MSG)

Even before He made the world, God loved us and chose us in Christ to be holy and without fault in His eyes.

–Ephesians 1:4 (NLT)

For I know the thoughts that I think toward you, says the Lord, thoughts of peace and not of evil, to give you a future and a hope. Then you will call upon Me and go and pray to Me, and I will listen to you. And you will seek Me and find Me, when you search for Me with all your heart.

– Jeremiah 29:11-13

Chapter 2
ANOINTING OF A SON

*"There are progressive revelations – if you walk with God,
you'll find there are things (which) will be unveiled this
coming year (that) you never thought about the past two or
three or four or five years."*
– Leonard Ravenhill

There are moments in all our lives where we find ourselves reading through Scripture a thousand times, and then at a thousand and one, there it is…something that we have never thought about or even considered asking ourselves why the Scripture reads the way that it does. We are all on a journey of discovering what appears to be hidden from us by God, but there will also be those things that have appeared to be unattainable, and yet, they were there all along. It happens to us all as we sometimes read through the Bible and we come across a verse or a chapter and discover that key word, that key phrase, or even that key name. We soon have our wheels turning inside of our thoughts as we come across something that is there in black and white (or red), challenging our thoughts, our ideas, and sometimes our theology. We come across that KEY that unlocks so many other things that have kept us from advancing in our purpose or destiny. It challenges us to question everything we have known or thought about certain topics or ideas. It forces us to dig deeper in the understanding of why or how. We find that we become more and more determined to grow in the revelation as it creates in us a hunger that can only be satisfied with the revelation of who we are in Jesus.

Honestly, it's such a profound moment in our lives when we have these WOW revelations. They are KEYS that unlock the doors that have been shut in our faces for years. These KEYS enable us to open the doors that position us to better understand who we are. They help us to recognize the potential we have in the purpose that God created us to walk in. They position us in our identities that help to launch us in our destiny. The difficulty you will soon discover will not be in how you proceed forward, but how these challenges will cause you to determine what you are willing to do with them.

Seek the Lord while He may be found;
Call upon Him while He is near.
Let the wicked forsake his way
And the unrighteous man his thoughts;
And let him return to the Lord,
And He will have compassion on him,
And to our God,
For He will abundantly pardon.
"For My thoughts are not your thoughts,
Nor are your ways My ways," declares the Lord.
"For as the heavens are higher than the earth,
So are My ways higher than your ways
And My thoughts than your thoughts.
For as the rain and the snow come down from heaven,
And do not return there without watering the earth
And making it bear and sprout,
And furnishing seed to the sower and bread to the eater;
So will My word be which goes forth from My mouth;
It will not return to Me empty,
Without accomplishing what I desire,
And without succeeding in the matter for which I sent it."

— Isaiah 55:6-11

The problem we face when we recognize truth in Scripture is whether or not we will allow it to advance us, or will we allow what we have always believed (or thought) to continue in defining us. Traditions and traditional thinking have limited many for generations. Not all traditions are wrong, as we should hold true the importance of many traditions. However, when those ideas or beliefs in those traditions become stronger than the truth of God's Word, we have a major problem. Through the decades of time, mankind has always had opportunities in the growth of revelation through Holy Spirit. However, man has also always been willing to reject those revelations because it challenged our way of thinking or living. As you continue to develop your relationship with the Lord, you will find yourself consistently being challenged to grow. It is the beauty of how the Father works with those whom He loves. He is never going to reveal the fullness of who He is in one glimpse. Rather, He chooses to show you more and more of who He is by revealing more and more of who you are. The challenge is ahead of you, just as the revelation that has always been in the written Word is before you. I want to encourage you to position yourself to receive what the Lord has established in your destiny.

Now the Lord said to Samuel, "How long will you grieve over Saul, since I have rejected him from being king over Israel? Fill your horn with oil and go; I will send you to Jesse the Bethlehemite, for I have selected a king for Myself among his sons." But Samuel said, "How can I go? When Saul hears of it, he will kill me." And the Lord said, "Take a heifer with you and say, 'I have come to sacrifice to the Lord.' You shall invite Jesse to the sacrifice, and I will show you what you shall do; and you shall anoint for Me the one whom I designate to you." So Samuel did what the Lord said, and came to Bethlehem. And the elders of the city came trembling to meet him and said, "Do you come in peace?" He said, "In peace; I have come to sacrifice to the Lord. Consecrate yourselves and come with me to the sacrifice." He also consecrated Jesse and his sons and invited them to the sacrifice. When they entered, he looked at Eliab and thought, "Surely the Lord's anointed is before Him." But the Lord said to Samuel, "Do not look at his appearance or at the height of his stature, because I have rejected him; for God sees not as man sees, for man looks at the outward appearance, but the Lord looks at the heart." Then Jesse called Abinadab and made him pass before Samuel. And he said, "The Lord has not chosen this one either." Next Jesse made Shammah pass by. And he said, "The Lord has not chosen this one either." Thus Jesse made seven of his sons pass before Samuel. But Samuel said to Jesse, "The Lord has not chosen these." And Samuel said to Jesse, "Are these all the children?" And he said, "There remains yet the youngest, and behold, he is tending the sheep." Then Samuel said to Jesse, "Send and bring him; for we will not sit down until he comes here." So he sent and brought him in. Now he was ruddy, with beautiful eyes and a handsome appearance. And the Lord said, "Arise, anoint him; for this is he." Then Samuel took the horn of oil and anointed him in the midst of his brothers; and the Spirit of the Lord came mightily upon David from that day forward. And Samuel arose and went to Ramah.

– 1 Samuel 16:1-13

Let's look at what has happened in these passages of Scripture:

1. The prophet Samuel is grieving over the sin of Saul.

2. God reveals to Samuel that He has a plan to anoint a new king.

3. Samuel gets the revelation of how to anoint the next king.

4. The elders tremble at the visitation of the prophet.

5. Jesse is invited to attend the sacrifice with *all* of his sons.

6. None of the sons are anointed.

7. Jesse reveals another son.

8. Samuel instructs Jesse to go get the son.

9. The shepherd boy is anointed to be king.

Now that we have the basic understanding, let's dig a little deeper here into what happened. Samuel is grieving over the sin of King Saul, in which God asks Samuel how much longer he would grieve over Saul because He (the Lord) had another king to be anointed. Once Samuel hears this, he asks God how in the world this would be as he knew that if Saul ever found out that Samuel anointed another, the king would have Samuel executed. However, the plan is initiated, and Samuel arrives at Bethlehem for a sacrifice unto the Lord. As he arrives, the Bible tells us that the elders of the city came trembling, wondering if the prophet had good news or bad. Once Samuel details why he is there, an invitation is given to Jesse and all of his sons. Once the group of sons arrive, the Bible says that the prophet saw Eliab and immediately thought this would be the next king.

Granted, Samuel never came close (other than thought) to anointing Eliab. But, we do have to recognize why this might have taken place. In the Scripture, we get the physical description of Eliab along with the correction from the Lord about not looking on the outward appearance of man. But why the correction? We have to remember that Samuel is the prophet that anointed Saul to be king, and Saul is described in the Word as a handsome man that stood head and shoulders above everyone else. The description of Saul sounds a lot like the description of Eliab. For one brief moment, Samuel saw Eliab and recognized that he looked like what was familiar. Thankfully, Samuel did not anoint Eliab, but we have to see the warning for us all here. Had Samuel anointed Eliab, he would have anointed the *new* thing based off of the familiarity of the *old* thing. There is a lesson for all of us as we have the tendency to declare what is God, based off of what already has been. And yet the Word declares that God is doing a *new* thing (Isaiah 43:19).

Eventually, Samuel goes through each son only to realize that none of them would be the anointed one. It's here that Samuel asks Jesse a very interesting question: "Are there any more sons?" Why would Samuel ask such a question? After all, the invitation was for Jesse to bring *all* of his sons. Better yet, why would Jesse *not* bring all of his sons? We do realize that the elders came trembling at the prophet just at his arrival. Surely Jesse wouldn't be disobedient to the request of the prophet. And yet, David isn't there. He is tending to the sheep.

We have to ask ourselves why a father wouldn't have one of his sons there for the sacrifice unto the Lord. It's too easy for us to say that he was tending to the sheep. We are too quick to believe or think that David was doing the job that someone had to do. We have to remember that in this day and time, when the prophet gave a specific instruction, people normally responded with following through as the prophet had requested. Can you imagine that you were given a direct instruction to bring your entire family to a sacrifice unto the Lord, and you made the decision to not be obedient to that word and leave one of your children behind? Who would do that? So, what if the fact that David is tending to the sheep has absolutely nothing to do with the work that had to be done and everything to do with the fact that Jesse did not want his youngest son there? At this point, we have to ask ourselves, why would a father not want his son to be a part of the sacrifice?

The answer: SHAME. When we look at the definition of shame, it can be defined as a negative or painful emotion that can be the result of having done something wrong to yourself or to others. We can bring shame into our lives by being caught in the act of doing something that is immoral or illegal. It is when shame invades our mindset that we can have our self-esteem, self-worth, or value as an individual stripped from us. When we do something that creates an environment of shame, it often produces embarrassment or humiliation when we are around certain individuals.

I believe that it's important to note that many individuals have been abused by someone physically, emotionally, or sexually, and because of that abuse, they have grown up with a deep internal shame that they are not responsible for. If you are dealing with shame because of what someone did to you, please take the time right now to allow the Father to heal you today through His perfect LOVE. God loves you and is not punishing you because of what others did to you.

Chapter 3
A SON'S TRUE IDENTITY

"God never uses anyone greatly until He tests them deeply."
– A.W. Tozer

Are your wheels turning yet? Have you found yourself wondering why exactly did Jesse not bring David to the sacrifice? Is the job of keeping the sheep that important compared to the invitation of the prophet to attend a sacrifice to the Lord? These are the type of questions that we need to ask ourselves when we are studying God's Word. We never study for the sake of questioning the authenticity of God through the written Word, but we must learn to study through the ability to ask questions that we may grow in truth. When you read those verses in the previous chapter, I pray that it began to stir something within you to recognize that not only was David a special anointed young man, but you, too, are going to connect the dots of knowing why the warfare over your life has been so intense. As David had a destiny to fulfill, your destiny is before you as well. We just have to come to a place of knowing that what was trying to stop David is often the very thing that is trying to stop you.

Save me, O God, For the waters have threatened my life. I have sunk in deep mire, and there is no foothold; I have come into deep waters, and a flood overflows me. I am weary with my crying; my throat is parched; My eyes fail while I wait for my God. Those who hate me without a cause are more than the hairs of my head; Those who would destroy me are powerful, being wrongfully my enemies; What I did not steal, I then have to restore. O God, it is You who knows my folly, And my wrongs are not hidden from You. May those who wait for You not be ashamed through me, O Lord God of hosts; May those who seek You not be dishonored through me, O God of Israel, Because for Your sake I have borne reproach; Dishonor has covered my face. I have become estranged from my brothers And an alien to my mother's sons.

– Psalm 69:1-8

David is the writer of this passage of Scripture and he gives us a detailed view of what his life was like growing up for him. He details how that those around him wanted him destroyed. He had to restore things that he did not steal or take from. He even details that his face would be covered in dishonor. Then he describes how he is estranged from his brothers and an alien to his mother's sons. There begins our question...are his brothers and his mother's sons not the same people? Well, let's look at what he said and place it into our understanding. David is describing two different groups of brothers. Think of it this way. My dad and mom were both previously married before they married each other. Through a previous marriage, my dad had a son in which we have the same father, but a different mother. Had my older brother's mom gone on to have more sons, my older brother would have had a set of brothers through his dad (we have a younger brother as well) and brothers through his mother. This is what David is detailing here in this passage of Scripture. The brothers are from Jesse, while his mother's son is part of a different set of brothers entirely.

What's even more interesting is the fact that David alludes to his face having dishonor. What in the world is he talking about here? Remember, in 1 Samuel 16, we saw where Samuel first saw Eliab and thought he looked like a king, but then God quickly corrected that thought. Then later in that chapter, we are given the description of David before he is anointed. One place we are given a description of appearance and told not to look on the outside, but then we are given a description of David, and he is anointed to be king. Why are we given that description?

Let's break down David's appearance. He is described to be ruddy with beautiful eyes, and very handsome. What is *ruddy*? Ruddy is the same word that is used to describe Esau in Genesis when he was born. When the Bible calls David ruddy, it gives us the understanding that ruddy meant that David was fair in his skin complexion, with red hair, and red freckles. Now, that may not seem like a lot, but think about where David is from. Bethlehem, which is in the Middle East. Most Middle Easterners are darker skinned, like a bronze or olive look, with dark hair. David looks nothing like someone from Bethlehem.

> Behold, I was brought forth in iniquity, And in sin
> my mother conceived me.
>
> — Psalm 51:5

In this passage David is revealing to us that he is the result of sin. When he tells us that he was brought forth in iniquity, it is the admission that David was the result of an improper relationship. Jesse would have either committed adultery or fornication with the mother of David. The word iniquity here implies that it is a sexual sin of adultery or fornication. Whether Jesse actually committed adultery or was committing fornication with David's mother, what this tells us is that David was a son that ultimately brought shame into Jesse's life. David was his son, but David would never be like the other sons of Jesse.

David was the physical result of illegitimacy. It's important for us to understand what exactly is being said concerning the word and idea of illegitimacy. We have a tendency to think in the terminology of being a bastard child when we hear "illegitimate," but this is not the case. Merriam-Webster defines ILLEGITIMATE as: not recognized as lawful offspring; specifically, born of parents not married to each other. In the natural, David shared the same father as his brothers, but because he did not share the same mother as they did, it brought him a lot of trouble growing up in the home of Jesse. David was a son, but was never treated as if he belonged in the house of the father. He didn't look like them and had to do more than them. His face was a constant reminder of the shame of the father. He was a simple shepherd boy that could only do certain things, but never be a part of the anointed things. And yet, he became anointed to be the next king. This is the point where we think that David's life would have immediately changed since the prophet Samuel had anointed him to be the next king. This would not be the case with David. When we continue to read about his life, we quickly see that he was sent back to the field to tend to the sheep. Jesse continued to treat David more like a servant of the house rather than a son who belongs in the house.

David was eventually summoned by Jesse to go to the battlefield in order to bring supplies and food to his brothers. When David arrived, his older brother Eliab became enraged with the presence of David and demanded to know why David left the sheep to come and watch the battle. Here was David with supplies and food for his brothers, but Eliab was declaring that wickedness was the reason why David was there. Soon David discovered that the giant Goliath had been mocking the camp of Israel and wanted to know why no one had done anything to stop him. David eventually found his way to the tent of Saul where he told the king that he would take down the Philistine giant. Saul attempted to place his personal armor on David before he sent him out to fight the giant, but David wouldn't wear the armor because it did not fit him.

It is my opinion that Saul knew who David was at this point in time. There is no Biblical evidence of this, and the following must be addressed as being nothing more than my opinion. (You do not have to agree with me on the following.) I find it difficult to believe that a shepherd boy, an illegitimate son, was anointed the next king by the prophet Samuel and no one told anyone else about it. Let's face it, secrets don't exactly have the ability to be secrets too often. I believe that Saul knew about David and ultimately that is why he tried to get David to wear his own armor. For years, we have had many leaders that become threatened by other people and those leaders will often try to get those certain individuals to wear what they were never called to wear. Sadly, today we have those kinds of leaders in the Church that are often like Saul. They understand that one of the easiest ways to get rid of the next upcoming threat to their position is to get them to wear what belongs to them (the leader/Saul). Saul would have known that if he sent David into battle wearing an armor made for him (Saul), it would destroy David.

Thankfully, David did not wear the armor! We know that according to 1 Samuel 17, David accepted the challenge of Goliath and he ended up killing Goliath by first hitting the giant with a stone from his sling shot. David continued to run towards the giant after he fell due to the stone. When David arrived, he cut the head of the giant off with the sword that was Goliath's. David then walked back to the tent of King Saul with the head of Goliath in his hands, declaring that the job was completed. David immediately joined the army of Saul, and when we read the rest of his life, we learn how it was filled with many ups and downs, and after Saul fell on his own sword, David took his position as king. By the way, it's important to note what 1 Samuel 17:54 tells us: "Then David took the Philistine's head and brought it to Jerusalem, but he put his weapons in his tent." This verse is an important key to remember as you continue to read.

David is the real-life story/event of how an illegitimate son became the one the prophet anointed to be king. The moment that this illegitimate son became a reality, it opened the door for the enemy to manipulate/pervert what had occurred naturally. Don't forget that Satan cannot create anything, but the very moment that God establishes something in the spirit or in the natural, this presents an opportunity of manipulation by the enemy. As with many things, the life of David became a great opportunity for the enemy to use illegitimacy to keep others out of their identity as a son. And yet, David wasn't just a shepherd boy who became the anointed future king. He was positioned and purposed for that moment. Just as you are.

I cannot reiterate enough the importance of recognizing that the enemy (Satan) is very wise in the manipulation and perversion of God's Truth. It's not that the serpent (Satan) came with a direct lie in the Garden of Eden when he approached Eve. It's the fact that he took what was truth and put a twist on what God had actually said. With a twisted truth (which immediately becomes a lie), Satan was able to convince Eve to do something that she was never created to do.

Now the serpent was more crafty than any beast of the field which the Lord God had made. And he said to the woman, "Indeed, has God said, 'You shall not eat from any tree of the garden'?" The woman said to the serpent, "From the fruit of the trees of the garden we may eat; but from the fruit of the tree which is in the middle of the garden, God has said, 'You shall not eat from it or touch it, or you will die.'" The serpent said to the woman, "You surely will not die! For God knows that in the day you eat from it your eyes will be opened, and you will be like God, knowing good and evil." When the woman saw that the tree was good for food, and that it was a delight to the eyes, and that the tree was desirable to make one wise, she took from its fruit and ate; and she gave also to her husband with her, and he ate. Then the eyes of both of them were opened, and they knew that they were naked; and they sewed fig leaves together and made themselves loin coverings.

– Genesis 3:1-7

I share this as a reminder because this has always been the strategy of the enemy. From the beginning of mankind, Satan has taken what God has established and used it to cause man to do or embrace what they were never created for. I want to encourage you that even though this is his strategy, never lose sight that he is just an imposter. Never the real deal.

Be of sober spirit, be on the alert. Your adversary, the devil, prowls around like a roaring lion, seeking someone to devour. But resist him, firm in your faith, knowing that the same experiences of suffering are being accomplished by your brethren who are in the world.

— 1 Peter 5:8-9

So… Let's keep going!

Chapter 4
ARE YOU THE SON?

*"There are many divine shifts taking place in the Body to
align people with great purpose. For those who seek the
Father, there will be revelation of assignment and destiny.
God is illuminating the path and revealing His plans."*
— Apostle Ryan LeStrange

When we fast-forward in time, we come to the
place where John the Baptist baptized those
who were willing to repent for their sins. As he
did this, he was a constant voice in the wilderness
proclaiming that the Lamb of God was coming to take
away the sins of the world. As John was baptizing, there
would have been a moment where he looked and there was
Jesus. There would be this amazing encounter that is
described in the Gospels where Jesus asked John to baptize

Him, but John tried to convince Jesus that He needed to baptize him. Jesus tells John that it had to be done this way, and soon John would do so. At the moment of the baptism we are told:

> Jesus came up immediately from the water; and behold, the heavens were opened, and he saw the Spirit of God descending as a dove and lighting on Him, and behold, a voice out of the heavens said, "This is My beloved Son, in whom I am well-pleased."
>
> — Matthew 3:16-17

> Then Jesus was led up by the Spirit into the wilderness to be tempted by the devil.
>
> — Matthew 4:1

We don't like it, but tests will come; they did even for Jesus. Immediately after the baptism and revelation of the Father identifying the Son, Jesus goes into the wilderness under the direction of Holy Spirit. Why did He go into the wilderness? To be tempted by the enemy. The enemy would tempt Jesus, but would do so in a manner that was very specific. Each temptation was against the identity of Jesus as a Son.

And the tempter came and said to Him, "If You are the Son of God, command that these stones become bread." But He answered and said, "It is written, 'Man shall not live on bread alone, but on every word that proceeds out of the mouth of God.'" Then the devil took Him into the holy city and had Him stand on the pinnacle of the temple, and said to Him, "If You are the Son of God, throw Yourself down; for it is written, 'He will command His angels concerning You'; and 'On their hands they will bear You up, So that You will not strike Your foot against a stone.'" Jesus said to him, "On the other hand, it is written, 'You shall not put the Lord your God to the test.'" Again, the devil took Him to a very high mountain and showed Him all the kingdoms of the world and their glory; and he said to Him, "All these things I will give You, if You fall down and worship me." Then Jesus said to him, "Go, Satan! For it is written, 'You shall worship the Lord your God, and serve Him only.'" Then the devil left Him; and behold, angels came and began to minister to Him.

– Matthew 4:3-11

Notice how Satan came with a direct accusation in his question, "If You are the Son of God"? When Satan couldn't get Jesus to deny His identity as the Son of God, he came at Jesus with worship in exchange of great power. Yet, with each temptation, Jesus responded with the Word of God. We have to recognize what the enemy was attempting to do with the denouncing of Sonship. Each attack was a personal attack of Jesus being a Son of God. As Jesus came out of the wilderness (with power from Holy Spirit), He went to the Temple where He pulled out the scrolls of Isaiah and began to read the very passage about Himself.

And the book of the prophet Isaiah was handed to Him. And He opened the book and found the place where it was written, "The Spirit of the Lord is upon Me, Because He anointed Me to preach the gospel to the poor. He has sent Me to proclaim release to the captives, And recovery of sight to the blind, To set free those who are oppressed, To proclaim the favorable year of the Lord.

– Luke 4:17-19

While He is reading from the scrolls, the Bible says that the people became enamored with the words that came out of His mouth. But soon after, someone spoke up and asked if this was the son of a carpenter (Luke 4). The moment that someone questioned who He was, the people became filled with anger and sought to have Jesus pushed off of a cliff. Thankfully, He would just vanish from among them.

We have to pay attention to the fact that the earliest attacks on Jesus had to deal with His identity as a Son. Before He does one single thing, He emerges out of the water at the Jordan River, and the Father declares Him to be the Son, and before long His identity as a Son is a major problem. When we continue to study the life of Jesus, we soon learn that this is a constant issue for Jesus. The Pharisees were consistently trying to get Jesus arrested on the grounds of proclaiming to be the Son of God. They could never succeed in that argument, but they tried. Even the disciples wondered about His identity as a Son at different times.

> The high priest stood up and said to Him, "Do You not answer? What is it that these men are testifying against You?" But Jesus kept silent. And the high priest said to Him, "I adjure You by the living God, that You tell us whether You are the Christ, the Son of God." Jesus said to him, "You have said it yourself; nevertheless, I tell you, hereafter you will see the Son of Man sitting at the right hand of Power, and coming on the clouds of heaven."
>
> – Matthew 26:62-64

Though this has been an issue, we do see in Matthew 16:13-19 where Jesus is revealed to be the Son.

Now when Jesus came into the district of Caesarea Philippi, He was asking His disciples, "Who do people say that the Son of Man is?" And they said, "Some say John the Baptist; and others, Elijah; but still others, Jeremiah, or one of the prophets." He said to them, "But who do you say that I am?" Simon Peter answered, "You are the Christ, the Son of the living God." And Jesus said to him, "Blessed are you, Simon Barjona, because flesh and blood did not reveal this to you, but My Father who is in heaven. I also say to you that you are Peter, and upon this rock I will build My church; and the gates of Hades will not overpower it. I will give you the keys of the kingdom of heaven; and whatever you bind on earth shall have been bound in heaven, and whatever you loose on earth shall have been loosed in heaven."

It's the first time that the identity of Jesus is confirmed to Simon Barjona, as he is able to hear the declaration personally from the Father. When Simon gets the revelation of who Jesus is, it unlocks the revelation of who he (Simon) is, Peter. Immediately after this, Jesus goes directly into the plan for His crucifixion and resurrection. Not long after Peter has this divine revelation, he quickly tries to convince Jesus that He cannot go to Jerusalem. Jesus then rebukes Peter for allowing the enemy to speak through him in order to stop the plan of the Father.

When Jesus is finally arrested, it comes at the hand of the Pharisees convincing Pilate that Jesus was professing to be king, while there was only one king (Caesar). Though Pilate tried to release Jesus three different times, He would be convicted and face death by crucifixion. He faced death as a king, not as the Son of God. When the Pharisees recognized that they couldn't get Him arrested as a professing Son, they changed their strategy to go after Jesus on being a king. The strategy worked, but the plan failed.

Now they came to Jericho. As He went out of Jericho with His disciples and a great multitude, blind Bartimaeus, the son of Timaeus, sat by the road begging. And when he heard that it was Jesus of Nazareth, he began to cry out and say, "Jesus, Son of David, have mercy on me!" Then many warned him to be quiet; but he cried out all the more, "Son of David, have mercy on me!" So Jesus stood still and commanded him to be called. Then they called the blind man, saying to him, "Be of good cheer. Rise, He is calling you." And throwing aside his garment, he rose and came to Jesus. So Jesus answered and said to him, "What do you want Me to do for you?" The blind man said to Him," Rabboni, that I may receive my sight." Then Jesus said to him, "Go your way; your faith has made you well." And immediately he received his sight and followed Jesus on the road.

— Mark 10:46-52 (NKJV)

Throughout the Gospels, we find where Jesus was called the Son of David. Why be called the Son of David? We have to remember that King David was promised that one of his offspring would rule forever. Jesus, according to Matthew 1:1 (the record of the genealogy of Jesus the Messiah, the son of David, the son of Abraham), is a descendant of David. Jesus was born in Bethlehem, the city of David. The declaration of Son of David is also a messianic title, in which Jesus never denied that He was the Son of David. At this point, we know that there is a constant attack on the identity of Jesus being a Son. Although there are clear declarations and revelations concerning the identity of Jesus, it's a constant battle to overcome.

Jesus also said, "I, Jesus, have sent My angel to testify to you these things for the churches. I am the root and the descendant of David, the bright morning star." (Revelation 22:16) Ultimately, Jesus is defining that He is both the creator of David and the descendant of David. The only person who could ever make a declaration such as this is the Son of God, which was made flesh.

Chapter 5
THE CROSS OF IDENTITY

"The Hallmark of an Orphan Spirit is the Survivor Mentality. The Mentality that says, 'I AM NOT LOVED' and 'RELATIONSHIPS DO NOT LAST.' This is the very spirit that God sent His Son to deliver us from."
– Danny Silk, Loving on Purpose Ministries

Now we come to the place where Jesus is on the cross, and He is facing His impending death, due to the reality that God is positioning Him for the full revelation of the identity of Sonship. I realize that for many, we still find ourselves asking, "Why is all of this happening?" It's important to remember that the concept of illegitimacy was opened up through the life of David, and David killed Goliath. And many are like, "So what?" David didn't stop with the killing of Goliath, but at the time there would have been four remaining giants left in the land. There was the brother of Goliath, and soon after, David ended up killing the remaining giants as well. 2 Samuel 21:22 says, "These four were born to the giant in Gath, and they fell by the hand of David and by the hand of his servants."

It's important to know that the giant race came to be when fallen angels (those who went with Lucifer/Satan) had a sexual relationship with women on the earth. When the women became pregnant, they would soon birth a giant race in which was half man, half fallen angel. The plan of Satan was to establish a giant race where the bloodline would be tainted.

> The Nephilim were on the earth in those days, and also afterward, when the sons of God came in to the daughters of men, and they bore children to them. Those were the mighty men who were of old, men of renown.
> – Genesis 6:4

This plan was to be implemented during the life of David so that the bloodline of David would become impure. We have to remember that Jesus was in the lineage of David, and Jesus was the spotless Lamb of God. Had the giant race done its job of tainting the bloodline of David, there would be no pure blood of Jesus through the lineage of David. But God had a better plan! David would not only kill a giant, but he would take out the remaining giant race. This ended the plan of the enemy for the bloodline. However, the moment that David destroyed that plan, the enemy manipulated another plan to do his work in destroying identities.

Take into consideration that David is an illegitimate son in the natural. Rejected by his own father and brothers, but anointed to be king. This illegitimate son has now given the enemy one of his biggest blows by taking out the giant race. What would the enemy do? Manipulate the natural for the attack on sons. The enemy has launched warfare on your identity as a son through a spirit of illegitimacy. The way that a spirit of illegitimacy works is through the roots of an orphan spirit.

For you have not received a spirit of slavery leading to fear again, but you have received a spirit of adoption as sons by which we cry out, "Abba! Father!" The Spirit Himself testifies with our spirit that we are children of God, and if children, heirs also, heirs of God and fellow heirs with Christ, if indeed we suffer with Him so that we may also be glorified with Him.

– Romans 8:15-17

God has positioned us to be sons, but it is an orphan mentality that will keep you lingering in wonder. So many people will go back and forth as to whether or not they are actually a son. A spirit of illegitimacy comes in to manipulate your mind with deception about your identity. It's important to really understand how this manifested in the life of Jesus. Every attack on Jesus was about His identity as a Son. The first thing that the enemy comes after is, "*If* you are the Son of God." Soon after, "if" was the questioning of whose son He was (in the synagogue). This would continue to be a constant theme throughout the life of Jesus. What the Lord is showing me and you, is that the enemy has been using this spirit to manipulate sons into believing they aren't good enough, nor will they ever be good enough.

Listen, contrary to popular belief, the enemy does not have a problem with you going to church. The enemy does not have problem with you calling yourself a Christian. The enemy does not have a problem with you occasionally praying, singing, running, or shouting. What the enemy has a problem with is your identity. Especially when you discover your identity as a son, and not just another church-attending, professing Christian. The moment that you understand who you are, everything changes. It's so much more than just being a Christian that attends church weekly.

A spirit of illegitimacy comes to rob you of your birthright. Satan uses a spirit of illegitimacy to create oppression in your life. This kind of demonic activity is constantly around, whispering lies about who you are and what you will never do. It's a manipulating spirit that convinces you that you will never be good enough. You will never sing good enough. You will never preach good enough. You will never be able to teach a class, much less preach a sermon. You will never be able to lay hands on anyone. A spirit of illegitimacy wants to keep you in your limitations. In other words, illegitimacy wants to keep you in the field rather than the palace.

Now that we are getting some clarity to what we are dealing with, let me encourage you with what Jesus completed. The Bible tells us in Matthew 26 that there came a point when the High Priest ripped apart his garments. This is a huge key in understanding what happened at the cross when Jesus declared, "It is finished." You see, the moment that the High Priest ripped his garments, it also signified that he was no longer the High Priest. If he was no longer in that position, then who would be next? Remember when Jesus was baptized by John the Baptist? John wanted Jesus to baptize him, but Jesus was direct in saying that John had to baptize Him. Why? John the Baptist was the son of Zechariah, the High Priest. Keep in mind that if John's father had died, the next in line to be the High Priest was John. However, John wouldn't live to see that possibility as he was later beheaded. However, John did baptize Jesus. I know you may be thinking, "So what?". We have to recognize that we are not baptized like Jesus was baptized. Jesus was never a sinner, saved by grace. The baptism of Jesus had nothing to do with an outward manifestation of an inward confession. The baptism of Jesus had everything to do with a rabbinical order. Jesus was a rabbi!

I know that many like to think that Jesus was more American than He was anything else, but that's not the reality. Jesus was a Hebrew, born in Bethlehem (in the Middle East). He was raised in a culture where young boys were given an opportunity to follow a priest into rabbinical school. When Jesus is called *rabbi* in the Bible, it's not a term of endearment. People did not reference Him as a rabbi because they thought He was a good teacher. He earned that title. Still struggling to accept that? Let's go back to the Temple where Jesus went in and straight to the scrolls. He opened those scrolls up and read from them. You have to understand that He couldn't just walk into a synagogue and take out the ancient scrolls, then read from those scrolls to the public, and finally take a certain seat in the place, unless He had every right to do so. He was a rabbi who had the authority to do so.

Need more proof? Remember the woman with the issue of blood? She purposely went after the hem of His garment because that garment would be a *tallit*, a prayer shawl. That tallit would only have been worn by rabbis at that time. We also have to recognize that as Jesus was being crucified, the guards fought over His garments. If Jesus was broke and had nothing of value, why would they fight over a garment of His? First of all, Jesus was never broke. Second of all, they fought over that tallit because it had a lot of value in it.

The High Priest had given up his position, and Jesus had been baptized in the rabbinical order. He went through the process of being a High Priest and at the moment of His declaration of "It is finished," He was able to say this because He would take His place as High Priest. "It is finished" was the term that the High Priest would say when the process of the sacrificial offering was completed and received by God. So, when Jesus declared this, He was ultimately declaring this from the position of a High Priest, offering the sacrifice to the Father, and the Father receiving it.

If that doesn't get you excited, let's think about the fact that Jesus is crucified at Golgotha, the Place of the Skull. For years people have often thought that the reason it is called the Place of the Skull is due to the appearance of the rock looking like a skull. However, let us remember that it is called Golgotha. When David killed Goliath, the Bible tells us that he brought the head (skull) of Goliath back to Jerusalem (City of David) with him and he buried it there. Goliath and his brothers were physically from the region known as Gath. Golgotha is actually broken down to be *Gol-gath-a*, which is understood to be Goliath of Gath. The place of the crucifixion is where David buried the skull of Goliath. This is the real reason it is called the Place of the Skull. Now, keep in mind that as Jesus was being crucified at the Place of the Skull, He would have been hanging on a cross in which His feet would be at the lowest point with blood running into the ground. Get the picture? Better yet, get the fulfillment of God's Word...

The Lord God said to the serpent, "Because you have done this, Cursed are you more than all cattle, And more than every beast of the field; On your belly you will go, And dust you will eat All the days of your life; And I will put enmity Between you and the woman, And between your seed and her seed; He shall bruise you on the head, And you shall bruise him on the heel."

– Genesis 3:14-15

Once Jesus took His place at Golgotha, this completed the final victory in overcoming identity. The problem: this has not stopped the enemy from continuing in his constant attacks against your identity. The spirit of illegitimacy has wreaked havoc on generations, but because God is revealing more and more to us today, we will overcome by the Blood of the Lamb!

"We have also been adopted into the family of God and are being sanctified, or made holy, because of what Christ did on the cross. Jesus' finished work on the cross accomplished all of these things for the people of God. We reap the benefits of His sacrifice, and we should praise His name for enduring the cross for our sakes."
– Dr. Tony Evans

Chapter 6
IDENTITY BATTLES AND STRUGGLES

"Those who walk in sonship are so grounded in their divine Father's affirmation that they can be satisfied serving in the background and can celebrate the success and attention others receive. The void in their soul has already been filled with the unconditional love of the Father."
– Joseph Mattera

Before I go any further, I want to detail some individuals in the Bible who battled with an identity as a son. With each of the names listed below is only a glimpse of their life. Due to the nature of their stories, I am unable to go into great details concerning their lives and the internal battle that they had concerning identity. It is my goal to share a quick glimpse with a name, for the intent to get you to take the time to dive deeper into their lives. Consider the names listed below as a starting point to your own research of how identity has been a major deal in the lives of many. This book isn't just about how important it is to look at David and Jesus, but also the lives of others through God's Word. Granted, the following list is not a complete rundown throughout the Bible, but a small sample to detail how identity has always been important throughout the time of mankind.

Cain

The Bible gives us our first issue over identity as the history of Cain and Abel reveals to us the root issue that Cain had with Abel. Though the two were brothers, it would become obvious that Cain felt like he could never meet the standards of his brother Abel. In the mind of Cain, he was convinced that Abel was the better son to Adam and Eve, and because he was the better brother, God would receive more from Abel than Cain. Cain's inability to recognize who he was as a son caused him to take from the identity of another.

Ham

One of the sons of Noah who was able to be on the Ark and survive the devastation of the Flood was Ham. It's interesting to note that Ham would be the one who would see the nakedness of his father immediately after the flood receded. It is often debated to what extent that Ham violated the nakedness of his father, but the point of bringing him up here is to point out that Ham allowed perversion to manipulate his identity as a son. Had Ham walked purely in the identity of a son, he would have known the boundaries of what was possible.

Esau

When we go back and look at the life of Esau we begin to see how identity as a son would be something that was not only stolen from him, but something he was also willing to give up. Esau gave up his birthright for a bowl of soup! The hunger of his flesh outweighed the hunger of the spirit man within him. Esau then attempted to restore his identity when he came back to the father for a birthright blessing, but what the father had already declared, was declared.

Jacob

Jacob is a classic example of someone who was doing everything possible to understand his purpose in life. Regardless of manipulation, deceit, or lies, Jacob was going to understand his life in some way possible. His identity would not come to be until the moment that he encountered God in a wrestling match, but until that moment in time, Jacob would spend years under deception in his purpose.

Absalom

Without a doubt, Absalom was one of the most messed up individuals we come across concerning identity. Here is the son of King David, and yet he is trying to use that position to overthrow the identity of his father. Not to mention the fact that Absalom was willing to get rid of others at any cost. Because he was unable to know who he was as a son, he lived a life that would be destined to take from others.

Peter

I know this may surprise you to a degree, but the truth is that Peter wavered in his identity. He knew that he was given the call to follow Jesus, but it would be a rocky road. Although Peter, known as Simon Barjona, was given the revelation of who Jesus was, he would also do his best to talk Jesus out of His purpose. Not only that, it would be Peter who denied knowing Jesus among the crowd, just before the rooster crowed. It was his inability to know who he was that kept him from knowing who Jesus was. That is, until the day of Pentecost.

John Mark

John Mark was not one or two of the disciples, rather I am

talking about the person who originally was supposed to go out in the mission field with Apostle Paul. Paul ultimately did not take John Mark because of the immaturity of John Mark. Paul knew that John Mark would cause more trouble and hardship, and that could potentially effect John Mark in a way that would forever alter him. John Mark is a classic example of how immaturity will keep you from your purpose. Immaturity as a son will limit you in what you can or will do. Thankfully, John Mark developed and matured as he eventually stepped out in the mission field.

Timothy

As the leader of the church at Ephesus, Timothy made many mistakes (like all of us), but it was to his benefit that he was a spiritual son to Apostle Paul. Many theologians believe that Timothy's biological father was not a part of his life, as Paul references his mother and grandmother in writing to Timothy. Whether or not this is the case, we do see that the relationship that Timothy had with Paul was crucial. Timothy would be corrected as a leader from time to time, and when we look at those corrections we can see where an identity issue could be part of the trouble that Timothy faced.

Again, these are only a small sample of individuals who potentially had some battles that surrounded their identity.

Whether it was a natural result or a spiritual one, we can look throughout the Bible and see where many faced difficulties that can be traced back to the revelation of their identity. Many of you today, as you read this, can also begin to relate or understand the root of your own troubles or concerns.

Granted, you can immediately think of individuals that you know on a daily basis who never truly embrace themselves in the proper identity that the Father established for them. Every time they begin to acknowledge anything, they do so from the perception of what they are going through or what they have previously experienced. Think about how many times you've been introduced to someone who was identified by their past and not by their current situation. Even our Bibles have titles above certain passages that detail people based on their past. It's the "Woman Caught in Adultery," the "Woman with the Issue of Blood," and/or "The Demon-Possessed Man." In the Word, we see this as a description detailing the verses, but this mentality easily carries over into our everyday lives. We introduce people to others by classification, but not by our true identities.

Though this is how we often describe people, it becomes a problem simply because we hang onto those descriptions, and they quickly become our own limitations. Many individuals are never able to get over the hurdle or challenges to those descriptions, creating a false identity and inability to embrace Sonship.

"Unfortunately, some Christians are having an identity crisis. They don't know who they are in Christ or where they are seated. Instead of identifying with Christ, they identify with the problems that confront them."
– Kenneth W. Hagin, Our Identity in Christ

Chapter 7
MORE THAN A
CHRISTIAN

"I didn't even know that I was always living for God, that I didn't know how to live from God. I was an achiever more than a receiver."
– Leif Hetland, Global Mission Awareness

Though the enemy has been attacking many with a spirit of illegitimacy, it's more important to know who God has created you to be. As great as it is to be called a Christian, that is not the goal, not the purpose. The word "Christian" is first used in Acts 11:26 – "and when he had found him, he brought him to Antioch. And for an entire year they met with the church and taught considerable numbers; and the disciples were first called Christians in Antioch." We understand that being a

Christian is to be someone who is Christ-like. But what if I told you that being a Christian is not what you were created to be?

Do you realize that nowhere in the Bible are we called to be a Christian? Actually, I believe that it is easy to be Christ-like. There are multi-million-dollar companies and business persons who are taking care of the widows and orphans a lot better than the Church today. These companies and individuals are doing Christ-like things, but that doesn't make them born-again believers. We have so many people attending churches and meetings trying to be Christ-like when the real challenge is whether or not you can be Like-Christ. To be Like-Christ is totally different than Christ-like. Think of it this way, Jesus not only went to the lepers and talked with them, but He touched them. I say that with a sincere heart to wonder how many "Christians" are actually doing more than having conversations with others. So, if we are not born-again to simply be called/defined as a Christian, then what are we? I'm really glad you asked. When you are born-again you are now defined as:

Sons of God

Because you are sons, God has sent forth the Spirit
of His Son into our hearts, crying, "Abba! Father!"
— Galatians 4:6

For all who are being led by the Spirit of God, these are sons of God.

~ Romans 8:14

"And I will be a father to you, And you shall be sons and daughters to Me," says the Lord Almighty.

– 2 Corinthians 6:18

As a SON, you automatically have a birthright. It's not that you are wondering whether or not you are accepted, but as a son you know that you have a relationship with the Father, and nothing can remove you from that relationship. You are not an orphan, but you are a son!

Joint Heirs with Christ

[A]nd if children, heirs also, heirs of God and fellow heirs with Christ, if indeed we suffer with Him so that we may also be glorified with Him.

~ Romans 8:17

Blessed be the God and Father of our Lord Jesus Christ, who according to His great mercy has caused us to be born again to a living hope through the resurrection of Jesus Christ from the dead, to obtain an inheritance which is imperishable and undefiled and will not fade away, reserved in heaven for you, who are protected by the power of

God through faith for a salvation ready to be revealed in the last time.

– 1 Peter 1:3-5

Therefore you are no longer a slave, but a son; and if a son, then an heir through God.

– Galatians 4:7

To be a joint heir with Christ means that we, as sons of God, will share in the inheritance of Jesus. What belongs to Jesus also belong to us. Christ gives us His glory, His riches, and all things. Do we get the fact that all that belongs to Jesus Christ belong to us, for we are joint heirs with Him?

Ambassadors for Christ

Therefore, knowing the fear of the Lord, we persuade men, but we are made manifest to God; and I hope that we are made manifest also in your consciences. We are not again commending ourselves to you but are giving you an occasion to be proud of us, so that you will have an answer for those who take pride in appearance and not in heart. For if we are beside ourselves, it is for God; if we are of sound mind, it is for you. For the love of Christ controls us, having concluded this, that one died for all, therefore all died; and He died for all, so that they who live might no longer live for themselves, but for Him who died and rose again on their behalf. Therefore from now on we recognize no one according to the flesh; even though we have known Christ according to the flesh, yet now we know Him in this way no longer. Therefore if anyone is in Christ, he is a new creature; the old things passed away; behold, new things have come. Now all these things are from God, who reconciled us to Himself through Christ and gave us the ministry of reconciliation, namely, that God was in Christ reconciling the world to Himself, not counting their trespasses against them, and He has committed to us the word of reconciliation. Therefore, we are ambassadors for Christ, as though God were making an appeal through us; we beg you on behalf of Christ, be reconciled to God. He made Him who knew no sin to be sin on our behalf, so that we might become the righteousness of God in Him.

– 2 Corinthians 5:11-21

As an ambassador, it comes with the natural aspect of a respected official acting as a representative of a nation. Ambassadors are often sent to a foreign land where the ambassador's role is to represent the official position of the body that has given the ambassador the authority. Think of it this way, in the United States we have a U.S. Ambassador that represents the entire Government of the United States.

Regardless of where the ambassador may be, they are representing the entire government. When you are an ambassador for Christ, you are representing the entire Kingdom of Heaven.

The enemy does not have any issue with anyone that calls themselves a Christian, but the moment that someone knows who they are as a Son, as an Heir, and as an Ambassador, they become a serious threat to the enemy. When you know who you are according to what God has created you to be, you are active in your identity. Being a Christian is not a bad thing, but it does come with limits when you settle in being just another person who attends weekly meetings in order to get your heavenly ticket punched. You were created for more and to do more! It's time for you to overcome illegitimacy and step into your identity!

"Saturate your mind with the truth of God's Word. It's filled with reminders of His unconditional love for you. He says you are fearfully and wonderfully made (see Psalm 139:14). He says that nothing can separate you from His love (see Romans 8:35). Don't let the enemy steal your identity. You are God's masterpiece. Believe it!"

– Joyce Meyer, Finding My Identity in Christ

Chapter 8
KEYS TO THE KINGDOM

"Some of you are frustrated with your own spiritual growth. You're pressing, you're pressing, you're pressing. But the Lord would say to you, remember, you are not the one who causes yourself to grow. For you are growing in My grace. And even though you can't see it with your eyes, know that I've done a deep work, says the Lord, and I'm continuing to do this work in your heart. I am rooting you and grounding you deeply into My Kingdom, deeply into My Son."
– Apostle Jennifer LeClaire

Everything that Jesus did in the development of the disciples and through His ministry on the earth had a direct purpose that was greater than that one single moment in time. We have to take into remembrance that Jesus wasn't only in position for the manifestation of the Savior for that day, but it was to fulfill the prophetic destiny of the Son of God. Where we often struggle is recognizing that we are a part of that prophetic destiny. It was never just about a plan or way of salvation. It was and continues to be about the reality of the Kingdom. I am not positive who originally said it, but many have quoted that there can be no Kingdom without a King. This statement is so true, and yet we have to know that within that Kingdom there is a purpose because of the King.

As great as it is to have a Savior for the sake of our eternity, it was never just about getting to Heaven. From the day of the birth of Jesus, to the moment of His ascension in Acts chapter one, Jesus was establishing the reality of His Kingdom in the earth. There will come a day that the Lord Jesus Christ returns to establish His physical Kingdom, but we need to understand today that Jesus did more than be raised from the dead after the crucifixion.

The disciples often struggled in the understanding of what Jesus was saying concerning the Kingdom, and likewise many today have found themselves in a state of denial at times with the Kingdom.

The revelation and purpose of the Kingdom have always been in the Scriptures. I want to encourage you that as you continue to read, open yourself to the understanding of what is written in the Word. It's not a matter of an opinion or an idea, it's actually written in the Scripture for you and me to discover.

> Now when Jesus came into the district of Caesarea Philippi, He was asking His disciples, "Who do people say that the Son of Man is?" And they said, "Some say John the Baptist; and others, Elijah; but still others, Jeremiah, or one of the prophets." He said to them, "But who do you say that I am?" Simon Peter answered, "You are the Christ, the Son of the living God." And Jesus said to him, "Blessed are you, Simon Barjona, because flesh and blood did not reveal this to you, but My Father who is in heaven. I also say to you that you are Peter, and upon this rock I will build My church; and the gates of Hades will not overpower it. I will give you the keys of the kingdom of heaven; and whatever you bind on earth shall have been bound in heaven, and whatever you loose on earth shall have been loosed in heaven." Then He warned the disciples that they should tell no one that He was the Christ.
>
> – Matthew 16:13-20

When Jesus gathered the disciples for this moment, He proceeded by asking them who "they" said that He was. He asked the disciples what others were defining Him to be. Jesus then asked Simon Barjona a direct question for his response and not what others were saying. By now, we know that Simon had the revelation of who Jesus was, but what we need to concentrate on is what Jesus gave Peter.

Keys to the Kingdom

"I will give you the keys of the Kingdom of Heaven." Do we really comprehend what this means? Not only are we given the keys, but given the authority to bind and loose according to Heaven. When you are walking in your identity as a Son, Heir, and Ambassador, it's then you truly realize that you have the keys to do something. Not just the ability to say things here and there. Not just the ability to do little things here and there. But to actually shift the atmosphere and change regions for the Glory of God.

In the Gospels, we see that while Jesus was active in His ministry on the earth, there would be a constant question surrounding Him concerning His Kingdom. The disciples and many others wanted to know when He was going to establish His Kingdom on the earth. Although there will be a day that New Jerusalem will take its place between Heaven and Earth, Jesus was not addressing that when asked. Each time they wanted to know when He would establish His Kingdom, He kept telling them that the Kingdom was already within them. What? Throughout the ministry of Jesus, He kept trying to get the disciples to understand that the Kingdom was within them, and not just in them, but they were also given the Keys to the Kingdom of Heaven.

The disciples actually came to Jesus and asked Him to help teach them how to pray. He responded with,

> "After this manner therefore pray ye: Our Father which art in heaven, Hallowed be thy name. Thy kingdom come, Thy will be done in earth, as it is in heaven. Give us this day our daily bread. And forgive us our debts, as we forgive our debtors. And lead us not into temptation, but deliver us from evil: For thine is the kingdom, and the power, and the glory, for ever. Amen."
>
> – Matthew 6:9-13 (KJV)

Here is a key for you and me. We know these verses by heart, and many will repeat one particular part as "ON EARTH AS IT IS IN HEAVEN." I quoted these verses here in the KJV because it's the only translation that we have today that uses the word *in*. (I am in no way implying that the KJV is the only translation to use. I am using this only for a reference here.) Look again as it reads, "IN

EARTH AS IT IS IN HEAVEN." I know what a lot of people immediately think, "Is there really a difference between *in* and *on?*" Well, think of it this way…when you go somewhere, you will probably go by car. But will you ride ON your car or IN your car? See, there is a difference. So, what exactly was Jesus trying to tell the disciples here? The will of the Father is that the Kingdom be released IN EARTH. What? Jesus isn't talking about the earth in which they were walking on. While the disciples (and many today) were looking for a physical Kingdom on the earth, Jesus was trying to get the disciples to understand that the earth He is referring to is MAN.

> Then the Lord God formed man of dust from the ground, and breathed into his nostrils the breath of life; and man became a living being.
> – Genesis 2:7

Jesus is describing the earth here in Matthew from the same root meaning of the dust from the ground found in Genesis 2. What Jesus was saying was that, "Thy kingdom come, Thy will be done in earth, as it is in heaven." In other words, due to the fact that the Kingdom is within you (Born-Again Believer, Son, Heir, Ambassador), you can obtain Heaven now! How is this possible? Remember Matthew 16? I have given you the Keys of the Kingdom of Heaven. You have Heavenly access! Because of *Whose* you are, you know *who* you are. When you realize that you have

Kingdom access, you will no longer have to live a life where you are constantly struggling in your lack. Your life as a son of God is not about surviving until you get to Heaven. There is more for you to obtain here, and now.

"When man fell from grace, he lost a kingdom, not a religion. He lost dominion over the earth; He did not lose Heaven. Therefore, mankind's search is not for a religion or for Heaven but for his kingdom."
— Myles Munroe

Chapter 9
EMBRACING THE
FATHER'S IDENTITY

"And if we ask how are we to know where our hearts are,
the answer is just as simple – everything which hinders us
from loving God above all things and acts as a barrier
between ourselves and our obedience to Jesus is our treasure,
and the place where our heart is."
– Dietrich Bonhoeffer

I want to remind you that the revelation that the Lord has unveiled through the Word all began with the vision that the Lord gave me about the father and son relationship. I recognize that there are many who will read this book and they will find themselves in a natural situation where they can relate to a father who was loving or one that was never present. Regardless of how your relationship was/is with your biological father, it's very important to know that we cannot put an expectation for the Lord to be the definition of a father by the reality of what we have through biology. Though my relationship with my biological father is an amazing one, I cannot afford to allow it to be how I view God to be a Father to me. It is the same with those who have no relationship or a bad one with their biological father. What the Lord wants to reveal to us as Father is so much more than what we can sincerely imagine. There is an abundance of grace, mercy, and love with Abba Father that we never truly understand, but that comes with more revelation as we grow in our relationship with Him. We cannot put a standard on the identity of Abba Father, but can position ourselves to learn more and more as each day we continue to grow as sons.

One of the important things that we must never overlook is the relationship that Jesus had as a Son, and a Savior. It's a dynamic relationship that Jesus made sure that you and I would not fail to remember why He died on the earth. With that said, let us continue in the unfolding as the Lord connects the dots with revelation. At this point in time, the Lord gave me another vision concerning a familiar passage of Scripture concerning a son and a father...

The Prodigal Son

And He said, "A man had two sons. The younger of them said to his father, 'Father, give me the share of the estate that falls to me.' So he divided his wealth between them. And not many days later, the younger son gathered everything together and went on a journey into a distant country, and there he squandered his estate with loose living. Now when he had spent everything, a severe famine occurred in that country, and he began to be impoverished. So he went and hired himself out to one of the citizens of that country, and he sent him into his fields to feed swine. And he would have gladly filled his stomach with the pods that the swine were eating, and no one was giving anything to him. But when he came to his senses, he said, 'How many of my father's hired men have more than enough bread, but I am dying here with hunger! I will get up and go to my father, and will say to him, "Father, I have sinned against heaven, and in your sight; I am no longer worthy to be called your son; make me as one of your hired men."' So he got up and came to his father. But while he was still a long way off, his father saw him and felt compassion for him, and ran and embraced him and kissed him. And the son said to him, 'Father, I have sinned against heaven and in your sight; I am no longer worthy to be called your son.'

But the father said to his slaves, 'Quickly bring out the best robe and put it on him, and put a ring on his hand and sandals on his feet; and bring the fattened calf, kill it, and let us eat and celebrate; for this son of mine was dead and has come to life again; he was lost and has been found.' And they began to celebrate. Now his older son was in the field, and when he came and approached the house, he heard music and dancing. And he summoned one of the servants and began inquiring what these things could be. And he said to him, 'Your brother has come, and your father has killed the fattened calf because he has received him back safe and sound.' But he became angry and was not willing to go in; and his father came out and began pleading with him. But he answered and said to his father, 'Look! For so many years I have been serving you and I have never neglected a command of yours; and yet you have never given me a young goat, so that I might celebrate with my friends; but when this son of yours came, who has devoured your wealth with prostitutes, you killed the fattened calf for him.' And he said to him, 'Son, you have always been with me, and all that is mine is yours. But we had to celebrate and rejoice, for this brother of yours was dead and has begun to live, and was lost and has been found.'"

– Luke 15: 11-32

In this particular vision, the Lord showed me the moment that the son had received the robe, ring, and sandals. The Lord asked me, "What do you see?"

I responded, "Lord, I see a filthy son covered in mud and pig waste, wearing a beautiful robe, ring, and sandals."

Again, the Lord asked me, "What do you see?"

Again, I responded, "Lord, I see a filthy son with his clothes ripped apart; he is covered in mud and pig waste. His hair is standing up everywhere and stiff as it looks as though it hasn't been washed in days. He looks like he would really stink, but he is also wearing a beautiful robe, ring, and sandals."

For the third time, the Lord asked me, "What do you see?"

Before I could respond to his question, I was quickly separated from the father and the son by a great distance. I was right beside them in the vision, but at this point I was at least three football fields away from the two. The distance changed how I saw the son this time because I was so far away I couldn't get a clear glimpse of the son, but I could still recognize that robe, ring, and sandals.

It's important for me to tell you that when the father called for the best robe, signet ring, and sandals, they would have all belonged to the father. So, when the father calls for them to be placed on the son, he was actually taking his own identity and placing it upon the son. That's where I realized in the vision that I could no longer see the son, I could only see the identity of the father. That's the point where the Lord spoke to me and said, "Your identity as a son doesn't stop there. Being a son is about taking on the identity of the Father."

When the Lord spoke this to me, I was immediately reminded of John 14:7-11.

"'If you had known Me, you would have known My Father also; from now on you know Him, and have seen Him.' Philip said to Him, 'Lord, show us the Father, and it is enough for us.' Jesus said to him, 'Have I been so long with you, and yet you have not come to know Me, Philip? He who has seen Me has seen the Father; how can you say, "Show us the Father"? Do you not believe that I am in the Father, and the Father is in Me? The words that I say to you I do not speak on My own initiative, but the Father abiding in Me does His works. Believe Me that I am in the Father and the Father is in Me; otherwise believe because of the works themselves.'"

Everything that Jesus did on the earth, He directed back to the Father. He never took credit for Himself, rather He always made sure that everyone knew it was for the Father. Jesus even said that He never did anything without first seeing the Father do it, nor did He ever say anything without the Father saying it first. If Jesus made sure that His identity as a Son was always connected to the Father, how much more should we recognize that ours is as well.

You will never truly love adulterers like you should, until you have the Father's heart. You will never truly love homosexuals like you should, until you have the Father's heart. You will never truly love liars like you should, until you have the Father's heart. You will never truly love the lost like you should, until you have the Father's heart. And the list can go on and on.

We have churches, hubs, revival centers, houses of prayers, and ministries that are filled with Christians who have become satisfied in just attending services in order to be a part of something. Sadly, many of those individuals remain defeated because they have become sustained in just making it, but not obtaining. It's time to see the Kingdom advance to new levels of glory!

"The truth of the matter is that the whole world has already been turned upside down by the work of Jesus Christ."
– *Dietrich Bonhoeffer,* The Cost of Discipleship

Chapter 10
YOUR DESTINY AWAITS

"Genuine spiritual knowledge lies not in wonderful and mysterious thoughts but in actual spiritual experience through union of the believer's life with truth."
— Watchman Nee

It is my prayer that as you have read this book, you have begun to recognize what possibly has been keeping you hindered for so long. From the beginning of time, identity has always been a real issue. However, when the enemy developed his plan to taint the bloodline of Jesus, it would be an illegitimate son to overthrow the plan of the enemy. When David took out Goliath and then the remainder of the giant race, it opened a doorway for a spirit of illegitimacy. By the time we come to Jesus, we see how illegitimacy was working against His life. It is because we see that in the life of Jesus that you and I are able to recognize that it's working in our lives today.

Though a spirit of illegitimacy comes to oppress you, you don't have to stay defeated. I am in no way implying that a spirit of illegitimacy has overtaken your life in such a way that you are unable to function. We have to understand that this spirit has an assignment to keep you limited in your purpose. It's a spirit that does just enough to keep you from walking in the fullness of your identity as a son. It's often so subtle that many will not even know it's active in their life because we have easily given it an excuse of why we aren't doing what we are created to do. We embrace the lies of this spirit as the reason we cannot be effective in this world. But I want to encourage YOU that God has more for YOU! Today, you have to know that all the lies and deception that you may have bought into have been from the enemy through a manipulative spirit of illegitimacy. Although you have not been doing what you were created to do, there is an opportunity for the Lord to redeem the time.

I also want to acknowledge the reality that some of you reading this are the natural product of illegitimacy and therefore that has naturally created hardship for you to overcome. Because of the decisions or actions of a mother or a father, you have battled in your life to be accepted, loved, and appreciated. What has occurred in the natural has given the enemy a way to torment you. Not only has the torment been something mentally, but it has affected many spiritually.

In a similar way, some are reading this book, but they are not the natural product of illegitimacy. And yet, while you have been reading, something within you has begun to have a revelation that the problems you have faced for years are the result of an open door for a spirit to torment you with these thoughts of a false identity. You didn't open a door with the mindset of taking on an illegitimate identity, but somewhere along the way you began to believe the lies of the enemy.

Whether it was natural or spiritual, whether you opened the door, or it came unexpected, the fact is that a spirit of illegitimacy has wreaked havoc on your destiny. All the things you were created to do, and yet you have not stepped into that destiny. It's time to overthrow this lying and manipulative spirit from your life. Don't get caught up in wondering how this has happened in your life, just know that it's time to deal with it.

I want to encourage you to take the time right now to repent and confess for allowing a spirit of illegitimacy in your life. How it came about in your life is not important at this moment, rather it's the fact that you have recognized what the root of the problem is. It's more important to repent (change your thoughts) for the disobedience that has been permitted in your life coming from the unwillingness to be obedient in what God has called you to do. I want you to take the time and spend a few minutes doing nothing but communicating with the Father, seeking forgiveness. When you have completed this, then spend the next five to ten minutes in praise and worship. The moment that you confessed and repented, you emptied yourself. This is why it's very important to now refill your spirit with some praise and worship. Turn on your favorite album or artist and spend that time being filled in His glory. Lastly, take the time to lay hands on yourself and begin to prophesy into your future. Declare the Word of the Lord, declare life, declare abundance! Declare, declare, declare!

It's critical that I also acknowledge the fact that someone could be reading this entire book, and they have arrived at this moment with a Holy Spirit encounter in which they have realized that they have never truly accepted Jesus as their Savior. You have come to this point with the understanding that you have never been born-again. Truth is, you will never overcome a spirit of illegitimacy without first being covered by the Blood of Jesus.

> Greater love has no one than this, that one lay down his life for his friends.
>
> – John 15:13

Jesus answered, "Truly, truly, I say to you, unless one is born of water and the Spirit he cannot enter into the kingdom of God. That which is born of the flesh is flesh, and that which is born of the Spirit is spirit. Do not be amazed that I said to you, 'You must be born again.'"

– John 3:5-7

Jesus said to him, "I am the way, and the truth, and the life; no one comes to the Father but through Me."

– John 14:6

If you openly declare that Jesus is Lord and believe in your heart that God raised Him from the dead, you will be saved. For it is by believing in your heart that you are made right with God, and it is by openly declaring your faith that you are saved. As the Scriptures tell us, "Anyone who trusts in Him will never be disgraced." Jew and Gentile are the same in this respect. They have the same Lord, who gives generously to all who call on Him. For

"Everyone who calls on the name of the Lord will be saved."

– Romans 10:9-13 (NLT)

If you have never accepted Jesus as your personal Savior, you've never been born-again…this is your day. Take the time right now to talk with the Father. Be honest. Be real. Be open. Share with the Father the sinful nature you are in, and know that as you do so, you are positioning yourself to receive. Declare that Jesus went to the cross, died for your sins, and arose from the grave so that you may accept Jesus as your Savior. Your sins have been forgiven and your life is covered by the Blood.

> Jesus, I ask You to forgive my sins, save me from an eternal separation from God. I accept Your finished work and death on the cross as the payment for my sins. Thank You for providing the way for me to have a personal relationship with the Father, Son, and Holy Spirit. Today, I have eternal life. Thank You for hearing my prayers and loving me unconditionally. In the name of Jesus, amen.

Finally, this word/revelation that the Lord spoke into me is not for myself. It's not a word that I claim as my own. I want everyone who embraces this revelation to go out and share with others about the spirit of illegitimacy. I want you to share the reality of the identity that others have. We can no longer simply be a people just attending a service. There is more for us to do before we die and step into eternity.

We have been created to release Heaven in earth *Now!* Don't wait any longer for a physical kingdom to appear, but know that the Kingdom is within the sons now!

"We ought to live every day as though we've come out of another world into this world — but with the power of that world still upon us. We should live and speak and move in that power, and have our whole being in Jesus Christ!"
— John Wesley

ABOUT THE AUTHOR

Ryan Johnson is mantled in equipping the Body of Christ to awaken the nations with a prophetic call of a rising Ekklesia. Ryan ministers with a prophetic voice of Revival and Awakening, with the demonstration of God's purposes in regions, individuals, and the Church.

On November 30, 1997, Ryan gave his life to Christ and never looked back. He immediately began working in ministry as a senior pastor of a small community church in May of 1998. From that moment on, he has continued to work in the ministry serving as a senior pastor, associate pastor, and student's pastor. Ryan and his family spent the first 11 years of ministry working in northeast Alabama and the surrounding areas. In the summer of 2009, they relocated to Virginia where they continued to serve the work that God had purposed in their lives. During that time everything began to change for Ryan as he began to fully understand his identity in the five-fold ministry. After serving in Virginia and North Carolina, the ministry relocated back to Alabama, where Ryan and his family currently reside. Ryan and his wife, Kristi, have been married for over 21 years and live near Fort Payne with their four beautiful children.

Ryan has been blessed to develop relationships with many great men and women of God who have taught difficult and real-life lessons for Ryan and his family so that they can continue to work for the Glory of God. It's these relationships that Ryan credits to his development as a leader who walks in authenticity, honesty, and integrity. Ryan strongly believes and walks in the understanding of accountability.

For more information or ministry scheduling, please visit his website at www.ryanjohnson.us.

REFERENCES

Preface, page v-vi – Leonard Ravenhill quote
Ravenhill, Leonard. Retrieved from
https://www.goodreads.com/author/quotes/159020.Leonard_
Ravenhill. Accessed 5 Nov. 2017.

Preface, page vi – Martin Luther King, Jr. quote
King, Jr., Martin Luther. Retrieved from
Goodreadshttps://www.goodreads.com/author/quotes/23924.
Martin_Luther_King_Jr_. Accessed 5 Nov. 2017.

Chapter 1, page 7 – Bill Johnson quote
Johnson, Bill. Retrieved from
https://www.goodreads.com/author/quotes/43395.Bill_Johnso
n. Accessed 5 Nov. 2017.

Chapter 1, page 14 – T. D. Jakes quote
Jakes, T.D. Retrieved from
https://www.goodreads.com/author/quotes/72902.T_D_Jakes.
Accessed 5 Nov. 2017.

Chapter 2, page 17 – Leonard Ravenhill quote
Ravenhill, Leonard. Retrieved from
https://www.goodreads.com/author/quotes/159020.Leonard_
Ravenhill. Accessed 6 Nov. 2017.

Chapter 3, page 27 – A.W. Tozer quote
Tozer, A.W. Retrieved from
https://www.goodreads.com/author/quotes/1082290.A_W_To
zer. Accessed 6 Nov. 2017.

Chapter 3, page 25 – Definition of "illegitimacy."
Retrieved from https://www.merriam-
webster.com/dictionary/illegitimate.

Chapter 4, page 37 – Apostle Ryan LeStrange quote
LeStrange, Ryan. (2015, February 6). "God is Aligning You with
Great Purpose." Retrieved from
http://www.elijahlist.com/words/display_word.html?ID=14383

Chapter 5, page 45 – Danny Silk quote
Silk, Danny. Retrieved from
https://www.goodreads.com/author/quotes/1707395.Danny_S
ilk. Accessed 7 Nov. 2017.

Chapter 5, page 53 – Dr. Tony Evans quote
Evans, Dr. Tony. Retrieved from
https://www.goodreads.com/author/quotes/2411.Tony_Evans.
Accessed 7 Nov. 2017.

Chapter 6, page 55 – Joseph Mattera quote
Mattera, Joseph. (2013, April 23). "The Difference Between the
Orphan Spirit and a Spirit of Sonship." Retrieved from *Charisma
Magazine*, https://www.charismanews.com/opinion/39229-the-
difference-between-the-orphan-spirit-and-a-spirit-of-sonship.
Accessed 8 Nov. 2017.

Chapter 6, page 61 – Kenneth Hagin quote
Hagin, Kenneth W. "Our Identity in Christ," Rhema.org,
http://www.rhema.org/index.php?option=com_content&view
=article&id=671:our-identity-in-christ&Itemid=256. Accessed 8
Nov. 2017.

Chapter 7, page 63 – Leif Hetland quote
Hetland, Leif. (2015, April 13). "Supernatural Baptism of Love."
Retrieved from
https://sidroth.org/television/tv-archives/leif-hetland/.
Accessed 9 Nov. 2017.

Chapter 7, page 68 – Joyce Meyer quote
Meyer, Joyce. "Finding My Identity in Christ." Retrieved from
https://www.joycemeyer.org/everydayanswers/ea-
teachings/finding-my-identity-in-christ. Accessed 10 Nov. 2017.

Chapter 8, page 69 – Jennifer LeClaire quote
LeClaire, Jennifer. (2017, January 25). "Prophecy: Press into the
Shift in Your Heart." Retrieved from
https://jenniferleclaire.org/articles/prophecy-press-into-the-
shift-in-your-heart/. Accessed 10 Nov. 2017.

Chapter 8, page 75 – Miles Munroe quote
Munroe, Miles. Retrieved from
https://www.goodreads.com/author/quotes/88114.Myles_Mun
roe. Accessed 10 Nov. 2017.

Chapter 9, page 77 – Dietrich Bonhoeffer quote
Bonhoeffer, Dietrich. Retrieved from
https://www.goodreads.com/author/quotes/29333.Dietrich_B
onhoeffer. Accessed 10 Nov. 2017.

Chapter 9, page 84 – Dietrich Bonhoeffer quote
Bonhoeffer, Dietrich. (1937). *The Cost of Discipleship.* Retrieved
from https://www.goodreads.com/quotes/895407-the-truth-of-
the-matter-is-that-the-whole-world. Accessed 11 Nov. 2017.

Chapter 10, page 85 – Watchman Nee quote
Nee, Watchman. (2009). *The Spiritual Man,* p.134, Christian
Fellowship Publishers. Retrieved from
http://www.azquotes.com/quote/488371. Accessed 11 Nov.
2017.

Chapter 10, page 91 – John Wesley quote
Wesley, John. Retrieved from
https://www.goodreads.com/author/quotes/151350.John_Wes
ley. Accessed 11 Nov. 2017.

Made in the USA
Middletown, DE
22 May 2021